Silchester

Jenny Halstead studied fine art and subsequently trained and followed a career as a medical artist, contributing to many publications, among them several editions of *Gray's Anatomy*. In collaboration with her late husband, she illustrated numerous books on dinosaurs and fossils. Her *An Artist's Year in the Harris Garden* (2013) was published by Two Rivers Press. This new book combines her skills as a painter and an illustrator.

Michael Fulford is Professor of Archaeology at the University of Reading where he was first appointed as lecturer in 1974. In that year he undertook his first excavation at Silchester. 2014 saw the concluding season of the eighteen-year excavation on *Insula IX* – The Town Life Project – which is the subject of this book. Excavations continue under his direction on *Insula III*.

ALSO PUBLISHED BY TWO RIVERS PRESS:

The Writing on the Wall: Reading's Latin inscriptions by Peter Kruschwitz
Caught on Camera: Reading in the 70s by Terry Allsop
Plant Portraits by Post: Post & Go British Flora by Julia Trickey
Allen W. Seaby: Art and Nature by Martin Andrews & Robert Gillmor
Reading Detectives by Kerry Renshaw
Fox Talbot & the Reading Establishment by Martin Andrews
Cover Birds by Robert Gillmor
All Change at Reading: The Railway and the Station 1840–2013
by Adam Sowan
An Artist's Year in the Harris Garden by Jenny Halstead
Caversham Court Gardens: A Heritage Guide by Friends of Caversham Court Gardens
Believing in Reading: Our Places of Worship by Adam Sowan
Newtown: A Photographic Journey in Reading 1974 by Terry Allsop
Bikes, Balls & Biscuitmen: Our Sporting Life by Tim Crooks & Reading Museum
Birds, Blocks & Stamps: Post & Go Birds of Britain by Robert Gillmor
The Reading Quiz Book by Adam Sowan
Bizarre Berkshire: An A–Z Guide by Duncan Mackay
Broad Street Chapel & the Origins of Dissent in Reading by Geoff Sawers
Reading Poetry: An Anthology edited by Peter Robinson
Reading: A Horse-Racing Town by Nigel Sutcliffe
Eat Wild by Duncan MacKay
Down by the River: The Thames and Kennet in Reading by Gillian Clark
A Much-maligned Town: Opinions of Reading 1126–2008 by Adam Sowan
A Mark of Affection: The Soane Obelisk in Reading by Adam Sowan
The Stranger in Reading edited by Adam Sowan
The Holy Brook by Adam Sowan
Charms against Jackals edited by Adam Stout and Geoff Sawers
Abattoirs Road to Zinzan Street by Adam Sowan

Silchester
Life on the Dig

Jenny Halstead & Michael Fulford

TWO RIVERS PRESS

First published in the UK in 2015 by Two Rivers Press
7 Denmark Road, Reading RG1 5PA
www.tworiverspress.com

ISBN 978-1-909747-08-1

1 2 3 4 5 6 7 8 9

Two Rivers Press is represented in the UK by Inpress Ltd and distributed by Central Books.

Cover design by Nadja Guggi with illustration by Jenny Halstead
Text design by Nadja Guggi and typeset in Pollen

Printed and bound in Great Britain by Ashford Colour Press, Gosport

For Amanda Clarke and Dudley Fishburn

Acknowledgements

We are very grateful to Amanda Clarke and the Silchester team for their support of the Life on the Dig project. We also owe warm thanks to Dr. Emma Durham for her help with selection of finds and to Dr. Lisa Lodwick for her contribution on the environmental section of the book.

We thank the Silchester Friends and the University of Reading for their financial support in making possible the publication and the exhibition of the completed works.

All finds are courtesy of the Hampshire Cultural Trust, with the exception of the following:

Grid p. 8; roundel, horse and eagle p. 9; Sarapis p. 32; glass p. 33; gaming pieces and awl p. 34; Nero stamp p. 39, keys p. 41; and tile p. 57, for which we thank Reading Museum.

Introduction

Prof. Mike Fulford, hat on head.

Opposite page:
The Droveway. The 16th century droveway that cuts across the Roman town: the only way to the excavation today for trucks, diggers and visitors. *Oil*

In the summer of 2013, Professor Michael Fulford of the Department of Archaeology invited me to be Artist in Residence at the University of Reading Field School at Silchester for the forthcoming year, 2014. I was to record all aspects of the dig in what would be its final year of excavation.

It sounded like an exciting project. I instantly accepted and drew a nine-week line in my diary in order to be on site to record the two weeks of setting up, the six weeks of the dig, and the final backfill and return of the site to pasture.

My first walk up the droveway from the church on a beautiful June morning, sketchbook in hand, was magical, with the sound of skylarks in an enormous blue sky. I was on my way towards this 'other place', this Roman town of *Calleva Atrebatum*.

The trucks started to arrive, making numerous journeys from the Hampshire lane up the droveway in clouds of dust, bringing JCBs to open up the second part of *Insula III* and double its exposed size. Then the loos and cabins started to arrive, marquees were erected, two walkways constructed, water turned on and tested. The campsite housed the set-up team, and I noticed one large tent that on closer inspection was carpeted throughout and furnished with a three-piece suite and chest of drawers – clearly an experienced archaeological camper! Equipment came out of stores and barns, and cabins started to be filled, food provisions stacked and WiFi connected. Silchester was suddenly part of the 21st century. The site was ready to function and to welcome the students.

Two walkways, used as viewing platforms for visitors, start to be constructed.

Under Canvas. The campsite begins to fill up and the 'village' starts to take shape. *Oil*

Opposite page:
Trowelling: each layer of soil is defined and everything within it other than the parent soil and gravel is kept and put in a finds tray. Special finds, typically of metal, such as coins and brooches, are kept separate and individually recorded in plan and elevation. The residual soil is thrown into buckets and barrows and tipped onto the spoil heap.

One of the two Open Days. Students and volunteers, appropriately dressed, greet visitors at the gate.

A young helper cuts and fills baguettes.

Sunday Morning. Students work six days a week with Friday as their free day. *Oil*

I came in as an artist. Mine was an independent eye with almost no knowledge of archaeology and no preconceptions about procedures or processes. I had to learn about them quickly in order to record the work and the play, the skills, the techniques and the enthusiasm of the students, volunteers and staff. I quickly realised that this was a community; the large campsite was like a village to which many returned year after year. As this was the last year, many volunteers who had been part of the dig at the very beginning (eighteen years earlier) returned to see its completion.

The appeal was that it was a specific project with a time limit. Lots of figurative studies – crouching, bending, stooping, kneeling, scraping, tapping and brushing, heads so close to the earth concentrating on their subject that it appeared quite spiritual as well as physical.

I was offered a certain amount of freedom to interpret, but I was reminded of the detailed work I used to do as a medical artist.

One of the challenges was to find enough colour at the site to make things appealing, so I had to learn to love viridian green, the colour of the cabins, which also offered structure to my compositions. Evening activities were fun, and so too the Open Days, when many workers on the site dressed up as Romans! Throughout the project my aim has been to try to capture the excitement of working on a dig as a student or volunteer, the work and the play, and the thrill of occasionally finding something special.

Jenny Halstead

The Roman town

Location of the excavations within the Roman town in 2014 (with sketch map of Roman town inset). Looking from *Insula IX*, southwards towards *Insula III* and the South Gate in the distance.

The inset plan shows the defensive stone walls of the Roman town as they still stand today, up to 4.5 m high and 3 m wide at their base. The complete circuit is approximately 2.5 km (1.5 miles) in length. The town is built on a spur of gravel at about 90 m above sea level.

The principal stone type employed in the wall is flint quarried from the chalk, of which the nearest source is about 10 km from the town. Every four or five courses of flint, laid in herringbone fashion, are capped with bonding courses of stone slabs, the stone coming from relatively more distant sources (approx. 50 km) such as from around Swindon, from north and west of Oxford and from the Weald to the south-east.

It has been calculated that the wall employed some 105,000 wagon-loads of flint and 45,000 loads of the other types of stone. The maximum load a wagon might have carried was about 500 kg, half a tonne. About 10,000 m³ of lime mortar were used in the construction. There were four major gates: North to Dorchester-on-Thames; East to London; South to Chichester and Winchester; and West to Bath, Cirencester and Gloucester. Another, smaller gate originally took the road to Salisbury to the south-west. Two further, postern gates are to be found to the south-east and the north-east, the latter opposite the amphitheatre.

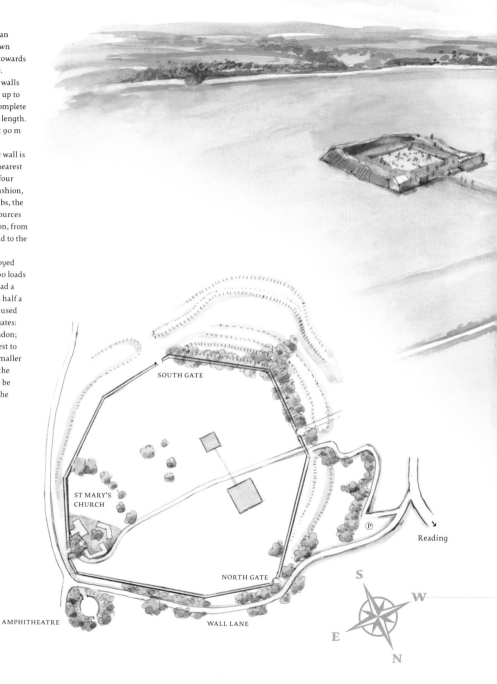

SOUTH GATE

ST MARY'S CHURCH

Reading

NORTH GATE

AMPHITHEATRE

WALL LANE

The Silchester Town Life Project

The Society of Antiquaries undertook major excavations at Silchester between 1890 and 1909 using a local workforce, mostly farm labourers. They excavated a regular series of narrow trenches diagonally across each *insula* (block) of the town. When they encountered the remains of a masonry building the ground was opened to expose its complete footprint. Gradually the plans of all the masonry buildings within the town walls were recovered.

The 'dig' in question is at the Iron Age and Roman town of Silchester, Hampshire, where, as the Silchester Town Life Project, excavation has been carried out over eighteen summers, 1997–2014, on a large area of one of the blocks (*Insula IX*) of the Roman town. The aim of the excavation was to trace evidence of the changing life of the town over 400 years and more: from its origins in the pre-Roman Iron Age in the later 1st century BC, to its abandonment sometime after the end of the Roman control of Britain at the beginning of the 5th century AD.

Today, the only clearly visible remains of the Roman town above ground are its massive defensive wall, built towards the end of the 3rd century AD, and its amphitheatre. Within the walls are grassy fields, but no traces of any buildings standing above ground level. Yet Silchester is arguably the best-known town of Roman Britain. Why? Towards the end of the 19th century it became the focus of a project sponsored by the Society of Antiquaries of London to explore in full a Roman town in Britain. Excavations in the 1860s and 1870s had shown that the foundations of buildings were well preserved and, as the site was open fields, with no pressure of development, it was possible to envisage a long-term project which could reveal the complete plan of the Roman town. At the time, Silchester within the Roman walls formed part of the Stratfield Saye estate and the Duke of Wellington was willing for the excavations to continue year-on-year for as long as it might take to explore the town in full. Over 19 years, between spring and late autumn 1890 to 1908, block by block, the plan of the Roman town within the walls was gradually revealed. Rather than leave the foundations exposed to the damaging effects of the weather, the trenches were backfilled at the end of each year and the site returned to agricultural use.

Insula IX in the 2nd century AD: town houses with tiled roofs in the background, their orientation still following that of the Iron Age town, not the Roman street grid; however, a thatched shop-cum-workshop in the foreground does align with the main Roman north-south street. Based on Margaret Mathews' reconstruction.

The excavations were a triumph! It appeared to archaeologists and historians of the time that they had recovered the plans of all the constituent buildings, so that for the first time for Roman Britain, and indeed, for the first time for the Roman Empire as a whole, the complete plan of a Roman town had been recovered. Iron Age coins record the town simply as *Calleva*, but in the Roman period the name was extended to include that of the local tribe, the *Atrebates*, hence *Calleva Atrebatum*. Excavations had revealed all the types of building that characterised a Roman town: a regular, rectilinear grid of streets divided the town into blocks with the administrative hub, the forum basilica, at its centre, and the distinctive, narrow-fronted shops (*tabernae*) clustering along the main east-west street. Most blocks contained at least one town house, decorated with the remains of mosaics and frescoes; there were smaller domestic buildings as well, and also Romano-Celtic temples and a possible Christian church. The public baths were located close to springs in the south-eastern quarter, while a large *mansio*, a hotel-like building to accommodate travellers on imperial business (*cursus publicus*) and their mounts,

From top left:
Grid-iron used for cooking food or warming drinks, described as a 'tour de force' of the smith's art.

Silchester-ware jar (coil built and tempered with crushed flint), 1st century AD.

Group of four Alice Holt (near Farnham, Hants) vessels (wheel-thrown sandy ware), later 1st and 2nd century AD.

Ceramics: drinking, serving and cooking at Silchester. Bowl and three beakers from an Iron Age well (note the maple leaf preserved on the small beaker), locally made.

Flagon, 2nd century AD, made near St Albans.

Large and small cooking pots, 4th century AD, made around Poole Harbour, Dorset

occupied almost an entire block close to the south gate. Although the final year, 1909, was spent exploring aspects of the defences outside the town walls, the project did not extend to the suburbs and cemeteries, or to the amphitheatre lying outside the walls to the east, which was not excavated until 1979.

If so much was already known about Silchester, why did we initiate the Town Life Project? The antiquarian excavations had told us much about the plans of individual buildings, but nothing about how the town had changed over time, or anything about its origins in the pre-Roman Iron Age. Excavation techniques at the turn of the 18th and 19th centuries were not developed enough to reveal either the complex stratigraphic story of a community that had developed over some 500 years or more, or that for much of its history the principal building material used was wood. Modern archaeology, however, provides us with the means to recover evidence of change over time,

5mm

Clockwise from top left:
Bronze roundel from military belt fitting,
3rd century AD, with the motto OPTIME MAXIME
CON/(serva)/NUMERUM OMNIUM MILITANTUM,
Jupiter Best (and) Greatest, protect (us) a troop
of fighting-men all.

Nero, coin of AD 64–68 showing the legend
IMP NERO CAESAR AVG P MAX, Emperor Nero
Caesar Augustus, Pontifex Maximus (high priest).

Silver coin of the pre-Roman Atrebatic king
Verica, showing the head of the Roman Emperor
Tiberius. The group of pellets under his nose are
an added Celtic motif.

The 'Silchester horse'. Bronze, of pre-Roman Iron
Age date (similar to the Uffington White Horse),
found in the Basilica by Rev Joyce in 1870.

The Silchester Eagle. Cast bronze, probably
1st century AD, found in the Basilica in 1866
by Rev Joyce.

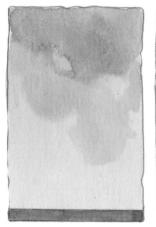

as well as of buildings in materials other than masonry. So, over 18 summers, and for six weeks at a time, with a team of up to about 150 working on site, an area of about one acre – representing about one per cent of the town within the walls – was gradually explored, layer by layer. Over almost the same amount of time and with a small team of about 20 workmen, the Society of Antiquaries had explored about 100 acres. Fortunately, as it turned out, their work was superficial, revealing only the later buildings towards the top of the stratigraphic sequence. The Town Life Project has provided much new information, particularly about the Iron Age and early Roman town, which was inaccessible to the antiquarians. Much more will follow as the results and finds of the excavations are analysed and brought to publication.

As the last archaeology of *Insula IX* was gradually excavated and recorded, a new area of excavations was opened in *Insula III*. The aim here was to re-investigate the remains of a building that the Victorian excavators had believed was a bath house. There was a strong possibility that it was a source of the fine building materials found re-used

AD 400

AD 100

AD 43 (Roman Conquest)
20 BC (Iron Age)

A stylised section of the Silchester *Insula IX* excavation trench, from the Iron Age up to 2015.

in early Roman contexts in *Insula IX*. These implied the existence of a hitherto unknown building, or buildings, of exceptional quality and early date in the heart of *Calleva*. Sure enough, the remains the Victorians had found in 1891 were early, certainly 1st century AD, but they were of a very large building, perhaps intended to be a grand town house, whose foundations, we discovered, continued beyond the area we had opened. Nothing we uncovered was consistent with the original interpretation of it as a bath house. How extensive is this early building and can we refine its date? There are indications in the Victorian account of the *Insula III* dig that early remains extended right across its area. Are they all part of the same building, planned to fit the *insula*? In 2015–16 we shall investigate further!

Life on the Dig came at the very last season of excavation of *Insula IX*. In the trench we were revealing the earliest occupation of the later 1st century BC, a triumph of the final weeks being the recovery of the full extent of one of the Iron Age halls that we had first encountered in 2010. At almost 50 m in length, it is the largest prehistoric building so far recorded from Britain. However, while the archaeology

Blue Skies. The site in full summer glory. *Oil*

continually delivered new knowledge of *Calleva* right up to the end of the last week of the season, *Life on the Dig* recorded an organised pattern and programme of work for delivering the excavation, with all its supporting infrastructure, which had become well established over the previous 17 years. Anyone visiting the excavation after an interval of several years would have noticed no difference in the way the excavation was being carried out – only the archaeology would have changed!

The annual cycle:

How the excavation was conducted

Behind the scenes before the dig

Each year, over the six weeks of the dig season, some 250–300 people took part in the Field School, with around 130 people, including staff, on site each week. Some stayed the whole time, but many came to discover what practical – and, in this context, Roman – archaeology entailed and stayed for the minimum period of one week. At any one time the majority of participants were University of Reading students. Those studying Archaeology for their degree stayed for four weeks to receive their basic training and fulfil the requirements of their degree, while those combining Archaeology with another subject like Ancient History stayed for two weeks. Interest from other participants in taking part would begin in January and places were usually filled by late April. Each year there were disappointed applicants. Organising the year's cohort was a complicated business: numbers needed to be evenly spread over the six weeks, and individual health, capacity and dietary issues had to be registered. The fields in the database were rapidly filled and there were always lots of questions to be addressed!

Managing a cohort of some 100 participants each week, the vast majority of whom had never taken part in an archaeological excavation before, required staff with appropriate expertise and, ideally, previous experience of Silchester and the Field School. Many professional archaeologists helped each year and negotiations for their temporary release from their workplaces on the one hand, and their temporary employment by the University on the other, also had to start early in

the year. We needed to ensure that we had the right people to manage the archaeology and its recording on site, the processing of finds (including the recovery of environmental evidence like seeds and plant remains), the catering, the day-to-day administration (including the management of the campsite) and the visitors. Over the six weeks, some 6000 people including school and society groups visited the excavation. Information boards and leaflets had to be prepared and visit guides briefed on the progress of the dig.

All of the organisation and day-to-day running of the Field School was in the hands of the extremely capable and utterly tireless Amanda Clarke, who was appointed by the University to assist the project from the start in 1997. Preparing weekly and daily rotas to make sure that every participant knew what he or she would be doing each day and that everyone spent time on each of the various activities of the dig was a huge undertaking, but it worked! Each day brought a new crop of questions and problems, but however large or small the issue, there was no anxious participant who could not be reassured and nothing which Amanda could not fix!

Jean Chapman, our caterer, is another long-serving member of the project. Indeed, she had first started cooking for our earlier digs at Silchester from 1980 onwards. Coping with the large numbers, some voracious appetites and the ever-increasing complexity of individual diets on a tight budget was a continual challenge, but one to which Jean rose admirably through the long six weeks of the dig season.

Though the dig is nothing without its participants, it could not proceed without a vast infrastructure of cabins, portable toilets, generators, marquee, rubbish skips, walkways for the visitors and the myriad of necessary, small, consumable items, from, on the one hand, hundreds of toilet rolls, to, on the other hand, pens and pencils for recording the archaeology and bags and boxes for storing the finds and samples. These, too, had to be ordered and in place before the start of the dig. Considerations of health and safety for the team and visitors

Protection from sun or rain? The extra small marquee is being erected near *Insula IX*.

Chairs lined up along the large marquee.

Opposite page:
Removal of the topsoil on *Insula III*, doubling the size of the trench from the previous year. Excavator and dumper truck working together. The soil needed to be quickly hand-searched for objects.

Starting in *Insula III*, the scaffolding poles are locked together by the construction team, while the set-up team weed a year's growth from the exposed surface.

The first batch of portable loos is positioned and the shower construction begins to take shape.

A Parking Place. The cabins arrive and are swung into position. *Oil*

Inquisitive Visitors. More tools and equipment are unloaded: spades, mattocks, buckets, etc. arrive and so do the locals. *Oil*

alike were paramount and a risk assessment had to be prepared and signed off by the University well before the start. Looking back over the whole life of the project it is a relief to reflect that, other than minor sprains, cuts and, in the very hot weather, heat stroke, no one on the dig ever sustained a serious injury.

Then came the setting-up week: cabins arrived and were put in place before being connected with the generator; the marquee erected; skips delivered; lorry-loads of equipment brought out from the University and nearby barn; internet access set up; the fresh water piping cleaned; the empty cabins transformed into HQ, kitchen, offices for data, finds and environmental processing, accommodation for the supervisors and the records, and for visitor services; the walkways for visitors constructed and safety checked; the Roman garden reinstalled; the excavation trench cleaned and the survey pegs reinstated. Only then were we ready for participants to arrive!

Students arrive

Below: Late Sunday afternoon 6th July and the students arrive, collected from the University or from the train station. Others, including volunteers living locally, come in daily.

No candles or electricity on the campsite, but solar panels can be found outside some tents to power a string of 'fairy' lights.

The shower construction allows solar bags to be heated up, ready to be hoisted to provide a warm, if not hot shower.

Opposite page:
Buffet Breakfast. Breakfast is served from 7.30 am, but only early risers get the hot toast. *Oil*

The dig is under way

Work commences: using mattocks to prepare an exposed section.

The site in full swing.

The Debating Society. *Monoprint*

Opposite page:
On Several Levels. Work on *Insula IX*: trowelling, brushing and recording, as well as removing the soil to the spoil heaps. *Oil*

Teaching

First Morning: teaching commences – explaining how to use a level to record elevations.

Flotation and sieving.

Seminars and lectures take place in the main marquee and also in the cool of St Mary's Church, a short walk down the droveway.

Opposite page:
Tools of the Trade: trowel and hand brush. *Oil*

Overleaf:
Thursday at 4.30. The Thursday late afternoon talk, a weekly summing up of what has been achieved on both sites during the last six days. *Oil*

26

Finalising the records.

Opposite page:
Top left: Drawing a plan and writing up the context card.

Hundreds and hundreds of trays waiting to be filled with 'finds' and CBM.

A volunteer marking the finds with the number of the layer in which they were found.

Awaiting Flotation: bags of soil samples. *Charcoal*

Processing the finds

Excavating within a town like Iron Age and Roman *Calleva* (Silchester) produces literally tons of finds each six-week season and the finds cabin is a hub of activity throughout. In the trench, the excavator puts every find – and this amounts to every object other than the parent soil and gravel – into a garden seed-tray, which carries the site code and the unique number assigned to the layer that he or she is excavating. That number remains with the finds through every stage of the processing on site, as well as during the research on the finds that takes place subsequently back at the University.

In *Insula IX* over the 18 years of the project we have identified over 16,000 different layers of soil, each of which has its own collection of associated finds. Those layers represent the stratigraphic record of

'Plank bridges' are needed over the trenches on *Insula III* to make an easy route for barrows.

Careful observation and reflection on what the dig is revealing are also an essential part of the process.

Opposite page:
The Presence of the Past: exposing the foundations for a colonnade opening onto the main north–south street; a dwarf brick wall links the individual column bases (*Insula III*). Oil

the history of this part of the town, with the earliest layers towards the bottom (the geological Silchester Gravels beneath any vestige of human settlement) and the more recent towards the top, the very top layer being the modern ploughsoil beneath the turf. What this means is that we can trace the changes in the lifestyle and occupations of the inhabitants from the late Iron Age, before the Roman conquest, right through to the abandonment of this part of the town after the end of Roman Britain, somewhere between the later 5th and the 7th century. It is through the finds that we can date the individual layers and, by grouping together those of the same date, we can build up a picture of change over time. We have now condensed those thousands of layers into six periods of occupation, the longest representing about a century, the shortest about a single generation of some 25–30 years.

10mm

10mm

The foot of a bronze drink-warmer or stove from Campania (an Italian region south of Rome) in the form of the Egyptian deity Harpocrates.

Military finds: *a.* Horse harness fitting; *b.* strap-plate; *c.* harness pendant; *d.* baldric clasp; *e.* strap plate.

What do the excavators most commonly find? Typically trays are full of pottery and animal bone, sometimes with a few iron nails. This is certainly true of the late Iron Age phase, but as we come into the Roman period, fragments of brick or tile – ceramic building material (CBM as it is known) – pieces of building stone and iron nails become common finds.

From time to time there is a cry of excitement when something different turns up. This may be the find of a coin or a brooch, or a fragment of coloured glass, or something more exotic like some of our very rare finds, such as the bronze figurine of Harpocrates. Originally he had formed one of the feet to support a small brazier or wine warmer, an exotic import from Campania in Italy, and the first of its kind to be found in Britain. Why the maker chose to make the foot in the form of an Egyptian deity is a puzzle, though Egyptian cults were gaining popularity in the Roman world in the 1st century AD (and

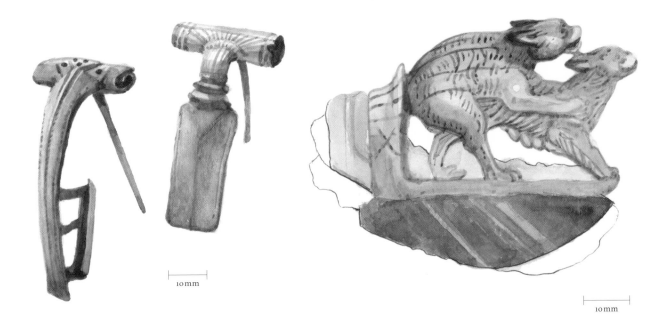

Brooches imported to Iron Age Silchester from the continent in the first half of the 1st century AD. *Left*: Nertomarus brooch. *Right*: Cravat brooch. Both would have been prestigious pieces much prized by their owners.

The carved elephant ivory razor handle (folded) showing mating dogs. Made on the continent in the 2nd/3rd century AD.

there is also an early find, a head of Sarapis, from Silchester). It clearly meant something to somebody in Silchester, because after the object was broken up for scrap, Harpocrates was spared the melting pot and eventually found his way into the foundations of a 1st-century timber building in *Insula IX*.

In the case of these special finds, a unique number, commonly known as the 'small find' (SF) number, is attached to them and, in addition to the layer in which they were found, their precise co-ordinates in relation to the trench grid and their height above Ordnance Datum are recorded so that we have the means to plot them two or three-dimensionally within the trench. We may, for example, wish to look at the distribution across the trench of all examples of a particular kind of object, perhaps all the Iron Age brooches, or a toilet instrument, or a type of tool.

Flint arrowhead. Early Bronze Age. Evidence of activity in the area of *Insula IX* before the Iron Age and Roman settlement.

The carved stone head of Sarapis, Egyptian god of fertility and afterlife.

Part of a pipeclay Venus figurine. The goddess was thought to assist domestic harmony just as much, if not more, than romantic love.

Pipeclay right arm; possibly a votive offering, broken from a larger figurine.

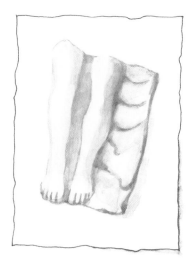

Beads found on the site over the years in various shapes and sizes: from 1st century turquoise frit melon beads, to small late-Roman glass beads in many colours.

Glass: usually found as fragments.

A small fragment from a millefiori glass bowl: beginning 1st century AD, a pre-conquest import to Calleva from the Roman Mediterranean.

Coins. *Top*: silver denarius of Antoninus Pius, AD 138–160. *Bottom*: a bronze 'barbarous radiate' antoninianus of the Gallic usurper Tetricus, AD 270–4.

10mm

Needles and hairpins in various sizes in copper alloy, bone and jet, 2nd–4th century AD.

Gaming pieces and dice in bone, ceramic, polished pebbles and glass. Knuckle bones were used for a game similar to today's jacks.

Samian ware. Black-slipped beaker made in the workshop (OF) of Libertus (LIBERTI) of Lezoux, in the centre of France, AD 115–130. Bacchic figures below the legend.

Spoons made from bone and copper alloy and a bone-handled leather-worker's awl, early Roman.

Opposite page:
Skeleton of a dog laid, as if in life, against the side of a late Roman rubbish pit.

Washing and cleaning the finds.

The trays are filled with the washed and cleaned finds and lined up daily to dry; each tray carries the unique number of the layer in which the finds were discovered. The commonest finds here are pottery sherds, animal bones, fragments of brick and tile, and iron nails.

Opposite page:
The Brush Bucket. A bucket of small brushes, nail and tooth, used for cleaning specimens. *Oil*

The trays of finds and the 'small finds' are brought back to the finds cabin for processing. The bulk finds of pottery, animal bone, stone and ceramic building material can be washed with brushes, and every day several 'pot washers' can be seen grouped together, working at tables, to one side of the cabin. Always retaining their unique layer number, the washed trays of finds are laid out to dry. Given the vagaries of the English summer, this may take several days and, as and when the inevitable showers come down, blue tarpaulins are pulled out to cover the orderly rows of trays laid on planks. Eventually, when completely dry, the finds are sorted into their various categories of pottery, animal bone, CBM, etc. Material bulk finds, typically pottery, are marked with their site code and layer number in permanent black or white ink. So, alongside the pot washers are others, their heads down at the table, patiently marking each and every sherd. Everything, every pottery sherd, every animal bone is retained, bagged and boxed, the only exceptions being CBM and stone.

a.

50 mm

b.

c.

d.

Ceramic building material (CBM):
a. roof tile (*imbrex*); *b. tesserae* used as borders of floor mosaics; *c.* flue tile with keying for plaster; *d.* tilers' (finger) signatures on roof tiles (*tegulae*).

Opposite page:
Nero stamped tile, found only at Silchester. The Emperor Nero, we understand, never visited Britain, but may well have financially supported the town's redevelopment; the bricks stamped with his name and titles are the evidence for such a project. NER(O) CL(AUDIUS) CAE(SAR) AUG(USTUS) GER(MANICUS).

A terracotta tile which had been laid out to dry, showing the impressions of a Roman sandal and an animal's paw.

The volume of these materials is such that we cannot afford to store them all. In 2014 alone we excavated 2.7 tonnes (!) of CBM, so we have to be very selective. CBM is carefully categorised into types, such as roofing tile (the *tegula* and the *imbrex*), flue tile from hypocaust systems, the flat tile used in wall construction, and so on. The numbers in each category are counted and weighed and then only specific examples are retained – those which are complete, typologically rare or distinctive, like the cutaway ends of *tegulae*, or which are marked, such as fragments with a stamp (in 2014 we found four examples with fragmentary stamps bearing Emperor Nero's name and titles from *Insula III*), flues tiles with their typical comb decoration, tiles with impressed human or animal footprints, etc. Once samples of the different clay fabrics of which the tiles were made have been selected, the remainder is discarded.

All artefacts of stone, which commonly range from fragments of querns for grinding corn into flour, to whetstones and architectural fragments, are kept. Unworked fragments of building stone, however, such as lumps of chalk or flint, are categorised according to rock type by our specialists with expert geological knowledge, then counted

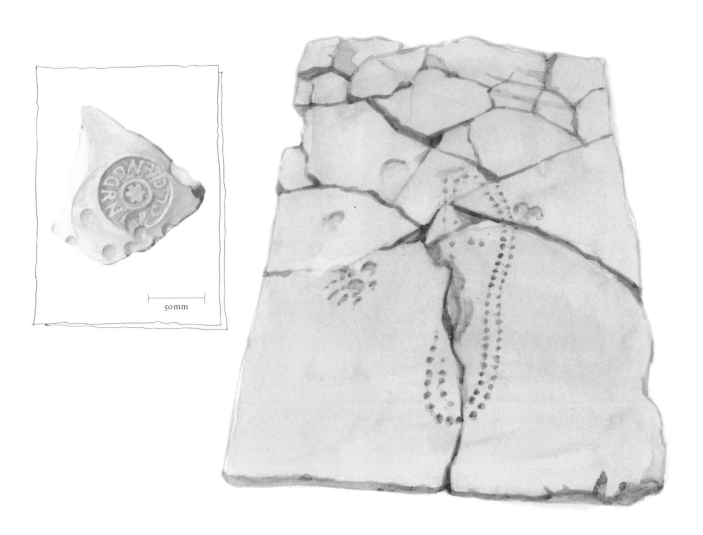

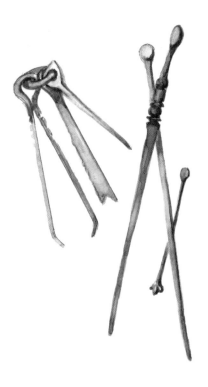

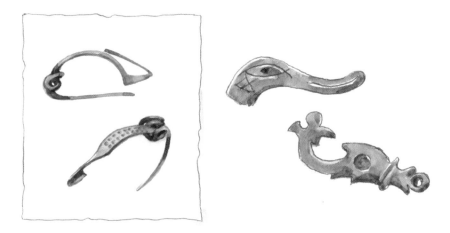

Toiletries: a toilet set of tweezers, nail cleaner and ear-scoop; long-handled copper alloy spoons for extracting perfumes and lotions from long-necked flasks.

Brooches: late 1st century BC to early 1st century AD British-made brooch with foot bent back on itself (*top*); a type of mid-to-late 1st century brooch introduced by the Romans and popular in new southern British towns (*bottom*).

Images of animals were everywhere! Small copper alloy fittings depicting a swan's head and a dolphin, probably from metal serving vessels.

and weighed. Once samples of each rock type have been selected for retention, the remainder is then discarded.

The treatment of the 'small finds' is different. Only robust materials, such as bone, pottery or stone, are cleaned on site. The metalwork, most commonly of copper alloy and iron, is air dried, but otherwise remains untouched. It is bagged with its unique numbers and boxed with silica gel on site to ensure the contents remain dry. After the end of the season it is taken for specialist cleaning and conservation. This reveals the detail of the objects; for example, most of our Iron Age coins could only be identified after they had been cleaned and conserved. Spectacularly, the figurine of Harpocrates was only seen for what it was after it had been x-rayed and cleaned. Much of the ironwork is routinely x-rayed; here, too, irregular, corroded lumps can often reveal unexpected objects!

All the finds data, whether the individual 'small finds', the records of bulk items like the pottery and animal bone, or the records of the discarded CBM and stone, is entered onto the project database. By the end of the final 2014 season we had almost 60,000 finds records, including over 7,500 relating to 'small finds'.

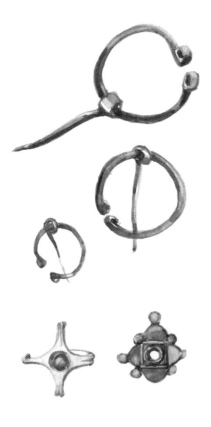

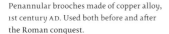
10mm

Penannular brooches made of copper alloy,
1st century AD. Used both before and after
the Roman conquest.

Continental-made copper alloy cruciform plate
brooch with tinned surface and red-enamelled
setting, mid 1st century AD. Enamelled copper
alloy decorative fitting from a leather strap,
2nd–3rd century AD.

Copper alloy rings and bracelets,
3rd–5th century AD.

Copper alloy ring keys, used to lock jewellery
caskets and sometimes worn on the finger as
a demonstration of wealth 'back home'.

Keys. Iron lift key (*left*); iron lever-lock keys,
1st–4th century AD (*right*).

After the retained finds are boxed up, they are taken into storage at
the University. Over 18 years the number of boxes has risen steadily;
there are now thousands in store! As each phase of the settlement is
researched further for publication, each category of find is studied
by an expert and all that stored material turns into new knowledge
about the economy and society of *Calleva*. Once the research on the
finds is completed, they are passed to the Hampshire Cultural Trust.

Processing environmental samples

Sketch showing the flotation tanks and bags of charred flots hung up to dry.

Sieving and bagging: sieving through gravel residues looking for bones, seeds and pottery.

Opposite page:
The Flotation Process. Water being pumped through the tank. *Oil*

Archaeologists can be seen here undertaking the processing and sorting of environmental samples, perhaps the less glamorous side of archaeology compared to digging, but equally rewarding for providing insights into the past. They are looking for the traces of food consumption, agriculture, metalworking and the Late Iron Age and Roman environment at *Insula ix*. Excavators provide soil samples from a range of features, from cesspits to hearths. The first stage is to break up these samples in the flotation tank. Plant remains, such as charred cereal grains, float on the surface of the water tank and are collected in sieves. These 'flots' are later examined in the laboratory under a microscope by an archaeobotanist. Samples from pits and ditches often contain grain and chaff of spelt wheat and barley, a few peas and flax seeds, and seeds of wild plants which would have be growing in the cornfields. These plant remains are all preserved

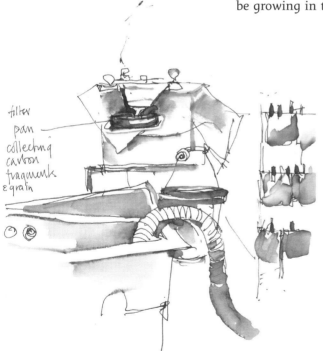

filter
pan
collecting
carbon
fragment
& grain

43

Students waist-deep in a rubbish pit dig out the sediments to be put through the flotation process.

Micromorphology sample of a pit section after being impregnated with resin and cut.

Opposite page:
Many seeds, pips and stones are found during the flotation process, giving clues as to what was eaten in the Roman period. Here the fruits and their pips/stones are shown together with enlarged actual finds (boxed).

Dried beans, peas, dill, lentil, barley, spelt, coriander and dill seeds.

by charring. Occasionally, rarer foods are found, such as olive stones and lentils.

Wells are also rich sources of seeds. The bases of wells have remained permanently under water for 2000 years, meaning plant material ranging from cooking waste to floor sweepings have remained intact. It was a late Iron Age well that produced the earliest evidence for the eating of olives, coriander and celery in Britain. The discovery of hay, flax seeds and cereal chaff from several Early Roman wells points to the presence of many animals within the *insula*.

Back at the flotation tank, once all the floating items have been collected the remaining heavy residue is wet-sieved and then sorted. Many small pieces of animal bone, fish bone and oyster shell, which would have been missed by the excavators, are collected. These are later identified by a zooarchaeologist, and tell us about the fish and birds eaten. Metalworking waste, such as slag and hammerscale, is also often recovered, as well as any coins, beads and even jewellery which have slipped past the excavators. Some plant remains are also collected during sieving. These are often heavy items, like hazelnut shells.

The smallest parts of the heavy residue (under 2 mm) are saved for sorting under the microscope. These include seeds preserved by a special form of preservation encountered in cesspits, known as mineralisation. Here, a form of fossilisation preserves any plant foods that have survived digestion. Samples from several Early Roman cesspits next to the north–south street have produced lentils, peas, figs, grapes, mulberries, cherries, plums, poppy seeds, celery, coriander, dill and flax seeds.

The many litres of samples sieved and sorted at *Insula IX* have provided a wealth of information for understanding the lifestyles of the *Callevans*.

Lisa Lodwick

Everyday life

The Red Scarf. *Pastel*

Assessing the data.

Recording and observing.

A pause for thought.

Opposite page:
Elevenses. Students taking a break. *Pastel*

A sudden rain storm and the site is cleared, in order that mud and possible finds are not lost on the soles of boots. So: a dive for the marquee, to do labelling and numbering.

Tools downed. Tea break!

Students starting to arrive for the Thursday afternoon talk and site tour.

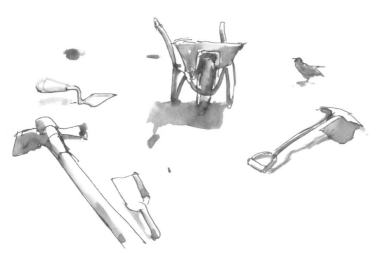

Student entertainment

Several visits by local groups of Morris Dancers who met up at the Calleva Arms. The students walked across Silchester Common for beers and dancing.

Pirate Night ritual. After locals have fired a live cannon the students make a dramatic charge across Silchester Common and storm the pub!

Pirates' Night Out. The Calleva Arms garden filled with pirates ... with hardly a cutlass in sight. *Pastel*

Dancing in the Dark. The Silchester villagers and Nick and Biddy West welcome the dig each year, lending it their barns, and, for this last year, arranged a hog roast and barn dance, as well as offering Mike and Amanda the 'Freedom of Silchester' medal. *Oil*

Opposite page:
Frisbee in the Amphitheatre. The Roman amphitheatre just outside the town walls, once the scene of many entertainments, put to excellent use again for Ultimate Frisbee. The long evening light, and the banks filled with an applauding audience.

Visits and open days

White Tablecloths. The Friends of Silchester are invited to a lunch on this final year of the *Insula IX* dig as an appreciation of their support. White table cloths contrast with the scene beyond. *Oil*

One of the two Open Days. Students and volunteers, appropriately dressed, greet visitors at the gate.

The tent is ready for the band to arrive.

Strike up the band!

Opposite page:
Visitors arrive and wait for timed tours to have the excavation explained by experts Prof. Mike Fulford and Amanda Clarke.

Children digging: buried treasure.

School Visit: Field Work. The children were taught how to trowel in a simulated trench, and found numerous pieces of pottery and tile, which they were asked to draw and guess what they might have been from or used for. *Oil*

Roman Visitors. On the walkway: ghosts of Roman warriors. *Oil*

Dyeing and Weaving. Invited exhibitors showing the processes used in Iron Age and Roman times for dyeing and weaving. *Oil*

The Roman garden

The Romano-British Garden, Sue Rowcroft busy at work. The plants, all of species known to have been found in Silchester or Roman Britain more widely, are stored over winter and replanted out each year, to show visitors either what was native and used, or what was imported and cultivated during the Roman period. The garden is divided into four sections: plants decorative, culinary, medicinal and ritual. *Oil*

A small selection of some of the plants and herbs used in the Roman world and still in use today: bay, rosemary, horse-radish, hyssop, sage, chives, garlic, basil, camomile, thyme, dill, lavender, comfrey and olives.

Behind the scenes after the dig

Within a week of the end of the dig, all the infrastructure, equipment, finds and samples had been removed. All that remained of the excavation were the trenches and spoil heaps and, in 2014, these, too, were soon gone. After 18 summers the excavation in *Insula IX* was finally completed; no more archaeology remained to be excavated from our trench and it could be backfilled. Over three weeks about 6000 tonnes of soil were pushed in and levelled, and our spoil heaps and trench gradually disappeared from view. The farmer reseeded the ground with grass and once again his cattle were able to graze where once we had painstakingly removed the soil, layer by layer, centimetre by centimetre.

Back at the University, the finds, records and samples were organised and shelved in their various stores, but it took up until the end of the year – a further three months of work – to ensure that all the remaining excavation and finds records, including the photographic record, were entered onto the project database. Only then could the

The final overview.

The taking down and removal of the walkways.

Insula IX: excavators and dumper trucks, five in all, work together to shift the heaps of soil banked up around the site. When the soil was removed the North Gate was suddenly visible again and a long-familiar local landscape was changed or gone. Eighteen years of painstaking work removing the layers vanished under 6000 tonnes of soil. A week later the farmer was sowing grass seed and then the cows reclaimed their field.

All Packed Up and Ready to Go. Everything is moved into the main marquee to be packed and labelled for removal back to the Archaeology Department. *Oil*

Opposite page:
Empties. Crates waiting to be filled. *Oil*

systematic analysis of the records, which underpins all the reporting of our work, begin. At the same time the metalwork and any other finds from the season requiring x-ray and conservation were taken to the laboratory in Colchester Museum. The last soil samples of the season had to be processed, the seeds and other botanical remains removed, and the residues scanned for microscopic finds. With the start of the New Year all was in place to write the first, interim reports on the previous season and the final cycle of the project's year was complete.

But this is also a time of beginnings: it sees the start of the research which leads to the publication of the results from *Insula IX*, with our first objective to work up all the evidence to reconstruct our earliest,

A terracotta tile showing a finger inscription of the Latin word *satis*, meaning 'enough'.

Opposite page:
Ave atque Vale (Hail and Farewell). After Mike's final talk summing up the 2014 dig, everyone was invited to walk on to *Insula IX* and collectively wave to the kite overhead.

Iron Age phase of the town, present long before the Roman conquest of Britain which began in AD 43; and it sees the preparation of plans to continue to explore the unexpected discoveries in *Insula III*.

What is exciting about both these projects is that they show there is clearly so much more to learn about the Iron Age and Roman town at Silchester. They represent small dips into a deep pool of knowledge waiting to be gradually released. Despite the work of the antiquarian excavators there are still hundreds of years of archaeology remaining to be explored within and outside the town's wall!

Two Rivers Press has been publishing in and about Reading since 1994. Founded by the artist Peter Hay (1951–2003), the press continues to delight readers, local and further afield, with its varied list of individually designed, thought-provoking books.